true love PROJECT

40 DAYS
OF PURITY
FOR GIRLS

sharie king
with clayton king

PUBLISHING GROUP
Nashville, Tennessee

Published by B&H Publishing Group
Nashville, Tennessee

Dewey Decimal Classification: 306.73
Subject Heading: GIRLS \ SEXUAL ABSTINENCE \
CHRISTIAN LIFE

Unless otherwise noted, all Scripture quotations are taken
from the Holman Christian Standard Bible®,
Copyright © 1999, 2000, 2002, 2003, 2009
by Holman Bible Publishers.

Also used: New International Version (NIV), copyright © 1973,
1978, 1984 by International Bible Society.

2 3 4 5 6 7 • 19 18 17 16 15

I praise God for being a faithful Father; in Him my life lacks no good thing (see Psalm 84:11). I would like to thank my mom for providing for me, and my grandparents for paving the way to my relationship with Jesus. Clayton, the Lord has used your love to heal my heart and make me a better woman. You are the most amazing man I know.

Contents

40 DAYS OF PURITY

Introduction

Tonight both of my sons had baseball games. My husband drove them to the field while I went to the store for team snacks and drinks. On my way, Clayton called to tell me we'd mixed up the game time and we'd have an-hour-and-a-half to waste in town. Our conversation experienced a frustrated silence because the past few months we'd been so busy, everything was planned to the minute. We didn't have time to waste.

"Well, what do you want to do?" I asked.

"I guess we'll just meet you at the field."

When I arrived, Clayton was pitching to Jacob in the batting cage, and Joseph skipped up to me with pleading eyes. "Mama, wanna throw the ball?"

My initial thought was, *No, I want to pout,* but the Holy Spirit helped me grab a glove.

When it was Joseph's turn to bat, I walked with him to the cage and realized how much I wanted to smack that ball. I looked at Joseph with the same pleading eyes he'd given me earlier and asked, "Do you care if I bat?" "Sure" he said.

I leaned back into my stance and felt adrenaline flow through my muscles as they anticipated the power I'd feel when the bat connected with the unsuspecting ball. After twelve hits in a row, my son's friend asked me, "Did you just finish your college season?" Laughter entered my soul because I hadn't played in twenty-one years. But, I decided to play with my kids a little and said, "Yeah. We just finished a winning season of 16 and 2." Exasperated grunts left both of my kids' mouths as Joseph said, "Don't believe her; she's one of those moms that jokes around."

Originally I was entirely frustrated by this mis-spent hour, but as I played with my family, I realized God was using this time to *make me play*. I didn't need to accomplish one more task. My soul needed fun and laughter, but I had to follow His lead to find it.

FOR GIRLS

God always knows what you need more than you do, but His ways don't always feel in line with your feelings. Letting the gospel define your purity doesn't feel easy, normal, or popular, so I've written forty days of encouragement to help you in this journey. But, it's up to you to listen to the Holy Spirit and follow His lead. As you walk this hard road, keep this in mind: I've never met someone who regretted saving their sexuality for marriage. I pray that you'll have the courage to leave the world's influences behind, listen to the Holy Spirit, and follow His lead.

The Chosen

But you are a chosen race, a royal priesthood, a holy nation, a people for His possession, so that you may proclaim the praises of the One who called you out of darkness into His marvelous light. Once you were not a people, but now you are God's people; you had not received mercy, but now you have received mercy.

—1 PETER 2:9–10

When I started middle school, it seemed like everyone left the simplicity of friendships on the elementary playgrounds and traded them in for a new form of entertainment: *relationships*.

I boarded the school bus where everyone buzzed about who liked whom. I noticed my reflection bouncing in the school-bus window. My permed hair and my shiny new braces were reflecting on the glass. As we approached the school building, I wondered how I was going to convince my class-mates to like me when I wasn't even sure if I liked myself.

I walked up to my locker, and my hands wouldn't stop shaking as I desperately tried to get the com-bination right the first time. In my peripheral vision I noticed stylish girls weaving through the hallways, turning all the boys' heads. They must have spent their summer reading magazines that taught them the secrets to looking great and standing out.

I wanted what they had: attention, popularity, and confidence. So I studied their clothes, hair-styles, mannerisms, and conversations.

After a few months I, too, walked the halls with what seemed like confidence. I was no longer on the bottom of the totem pole, and the group I wanted to join started to let me into their conversations. But it wasn't what I expected.

I listened as the opinions of my "friends" changed about one another with each passing day, situation, or conversation. And I was sure this was true of their conversations about me. The power of my new style didn't earn me the attention I wanted. Boys complimented me with a slap on the rear instead of a love letter or dinner.

I was trying to fill the natural human desire to be noticed, to find affection and love through friendship, but I kept coming up empty. I was in a danger zone. My heart was beating to the beat of blinking yellow caution lights.

The caution in my soul was a warning. As a young Christian, I'd come to a crossroads in my faith. My pounding heart was Jesus asking, "Will you let other people dictate whom you become, or will you become the woman I've created you to be?"

So, ladies, my question is this: If we know the God of the universe chose us to be His children, why would we ever let a mere person define who we are or whom we will become?

When you're looking at your reflection on that bus, feeling like nothing, remember Jesus gave up His life to give yours value. When people like you one day only to reject you the next, remember Jesus' love doesn't flip-flop. He doesn't ask to be your friend one day, only to abandon you the next. He is faithful, and His love is permanent and eternal.

You've been chosen by the God of the universe.
Will you choose Him?

The Challenge

Let us run with endurance the race that lies before us, keeping our eyes on Jesus, the source and perfecter of our faith.

—HEBREWS 12:1–2

Most of us have been told that Jesus' love is faithfully permanent. But the test of whether we believe it comes in that moment when we feel like we've failed Jesus. All of a sudden the door of doubt opens in our hearts, and uneasy thoughts creep through the cracks.

"He loved me before, but does He love me now? Maybe if I _____ (fill in the blank), I can prove my love, and He will take me back."

The more we doubt, the farther we run from the truth. The truth is: He promised to love you permanently. The challenge is to believe this is true when all the messages around us scream just the opposite.

I was excited to wake up the morning Clayton and I were to shoot the video teachings for the True Love Project until I looked in the mirror.

Ugh! I thought. *Why didn't anyone tell my body that I was only supposed to break out as a teenager?*

LifeWay had someone on set to do hair and makeup, but I panicked anyway. I didn't even want the makeup artist to see the giant protrusion on my face, much less all the lovely audiences who would watch the videos for years to come.

Thankfully I had my HD concealer, made to cover those imperfections you don't want people to see when shooting high-definition film. Still, as the sweet lady applied layer after layer of high-coverage foundation, assuring me no one would notice, I knew better. For the next twenty years, people would notice the flaw beneath the cover-up.

American Christianity dictates that we need to be like Jesus. But if you're like me, I more consistently mess up and make mistakes than count my successes.

Doesn't God know it's impossible to live just like Jesus?

Yes.

Then why does He expect us to?

He doesn't.

In the book of Matthew, Jesus talks to a group of religious leaders. These guys thought that keeping the law earned them brownie points with God. Jesus said to them, "Woe to you, scribes and Pharisees, hypocrites! You are like whitewashed tombs, which appear beautiful on the outside, but inside are full of dead men's bones and every impurity" (Matthew 23:27).

I'm sure these Pharisees felt God expected them to be perfect, so they created law upon law to safeguard them from making mistakes. Just like us, they were trying to live up to an impossible standard. In His confrontation, Jesus is saying, "Hey guys, you may think all these good things you are doing are throwing Me off, but nothing is invisible to Me. I see your messed up heart, and I wish you'd stop trying to make things right and start trusting Me."

We can live in intimidation and fear, hoping that one day we will do enough to please God. Or we can live a life of intimacy where we stop covering over our sin and let Him take care of it.

If you're trying to perfect yourself, you're taking on a job only Jesus can do. Your perfection was a by-product of your salvation. He's already made you perfect even though you may not feel like it today—or any other day.

When I mess up, fail, or am frustrated, I thank Jesus that one day I will no longer sin. On the day I see Him, He will put a white robe on me and erase all of my struggles and disappointments. He will look into my eyes and say, "Well done"—not because I was able to accomplish anything revolutionary but because I didn't stop trying to love Him every time I wanted to give up.

This is your challenge too. Will you love and trust Jesus in the midst of your failure, knowing that He—*not* your behavior—brings about your perfection?

DAY
3

The Choice

Give, and it will be given to you; a good
measure—pressed down, shaken together,
and running over—will be poured into
your lap. For with the measure you use,
it will be measured back to you.

—LUKE 6:38

He made me dinner, then got down on one knee and asked me to marry him. I wasn't shocked, but I was a little surprised. "The question" came sooner than expected. I'd waited my entire life for this question, but now I was scared to answer. My mouth was empty and my tongue uneasy, but soon a whispered and wavering yes came out.

I sat there a little disappointed because I thought this moment would make me a lot happier, but for some reason it felt wrong. I made the moment even more complicated when I asked him, "What did my parents say when you asked them if you could marry me?"

Now he became tense and nervous as he explained, "They wanted me to wait, but I already had things planned."

I went into the other room and spent the next thirty minutes crying with my mom on the phone. She told me that she didn't want it to happen like this. The magical night I had dreamed of was now becoming a nightmare. But we had to put on smiles as we announced our happy decision to all the friends who were waiting with congratulations.

The next few months I experienced a mixture of happiness and confusion. He wasn't a bad guy, and

I liked the idea of being securely married after college. But my mom's concern was soon joined with that of my grandparents. The next few months were filled with red flags and doubt, but I was afraid to disappoint everyone—and to be alone.

In my misery God spoke clearly to me through a book I received in the mail. I knew He was telling me to let it go. Afraid, I sat down with my fiancé the next week and broke my word, broke his heart, and lost a lot of friends in one day.

It was the loneliest time of my life. I questioned my decision every time I thought about my future and every time I passed him on campus. I cried myself to sleep each night, choosing to trust that God had my best in mind but never quite sure.

The thing is, trust is not something that comes natural to me. I had two stepfathers who were abusive, so naturally I gravitate toward caution and skepticism. I was eleven when I started following Jesus, and while I could feel His love, my soul had a hard time understanding why. I didn't feel special or worthy so I assumed His love originated from pity or obligation. My soul was eager to prove I wasn't a disappointment and I was worthy of His death. I tried to prove myself for thirteen years, until I finally realized God didn't want something from me but offered something *for* me.

Look at that Scripture from Luke 6:38 again. At first glance this skeptical girl sees the word *give* and thinks, *Oh yeah. Of course God is telling me to give Him something.* And a deep part of my soul feels like He is stealing from me. But if we look a little deeper, He tells us that so much more will be given back, "pressed down, shaken together, and running over"!

If He's asking you to give something, His plan is to give so much more back to you. When I gave up this engagement, God not only provided a husband who has exceeded all my expectations, but He taught me to trust Him more than I ever had.

God is the ultimate Gift Giver.

Your future depends on your choice to trust Him. You may not feel ready, but if you're willing, He will take it!

DAY 4

Better Than Sin

But everything that was a gain to me, I have considered to be a loss because of Christ. More than that, I also consider everything to be a loss in view of the surpassing value of knowing Christ Jesus my Lord. Because of Him I have suffered the loss of all things and consider them filth, so that I may gain Christ.

—Philippians 3:7–8

Sometimes it stinks to be "the good girl." It seems like everyone around you is having fun, and all you have are your wise choices and boring life.

No one asks you to the parties anymore because you've already said, "No, I don't drink." At one time your answer felt like a victory, but now you're feeling left out, lonely.

Boys don't ask you out because you won't have sex like all the other girls. You should be thankful not to have the temptation, but instead you feel unattractive and unpursued.

Is God really worth everything I am giving up? you wonder. *Will this sacrifice be worth it one day, or will I end up a bitter old woman?*

I understand your struggles. I've had them too. Sometimes I was confident and faithful, but others times I compromised. Rejection led me to make some popular but unwise decisions.

I wanted to see if sin would look as good on me as it did on other people, so I went to a party at a friend's house. I thought it would be a safe environment because her parents were chaperoning. But they were the ones who offered me my first drink. I said no the first few times, but eventually I was walking around clutching a beer.

A good friend tried to hold me accountable. "I thought you weren't going to drink?" This was my first warning from God. But I blew it off. Mistake number one.

Three beers later I found myself kissing a boy whose name I didn't know. Shocked at my own behavior combined with a sick feeling in my stomach became warning number two. Warning number three came immediately after. God spoke to me quietly, "Sharie, this isn't you." I didn't ignore God this time.

I left the party area and crept up to my friend's room. I wanted my own bed, but because I'd been drinking, I spent the night in her dark secluded closet. The "fun" outside didn't carry the same enticement. I was coming to a deeper understanding that my relationship with Christ was better than sin. You will never understand how wonderful God is until you believe sin is worthless. In other words sin has no place of value in your life. You have to die to the parts of you that are not like Him because:

• Each time you die to sin, you know your soul has been transformed by God using the power that raised Jesus from the dead.

- Each time you access His power, you will understand a little bit more what it means to be dead to sin and alive in Christ.
- Each time you decide that Jesus is better than sin, your bond with Him grows deeper.

It's up to you. Will you build your fellowship with Christ or sacrifice it for sin's sake?

DAY 5

Conditional Intimacy

I said to Yahweh, "You are my Lord;
I have nothing good besides You."

—Psalm 16:2

Joseph's brothers thought he was an arrogant punk, and they were jealous that their father gave him preferential treatment. So one day they sold him as a slave to a caravan headed for Egypt. His journey led him to serve under Pharaoh, who noticed his hard work and eventually gave him a promotion to serving as his right-hand man. But tragedy came again when Pharaoh's wife accused Joseph of seducing her. Though innocent, Joseph was thrown into prison.

Maybe Joseph had an unconquerable spirit, or perhaps he was simply stir-crazy. For whatever reason he started working hard again and earned a valuable position in prison. He became known and noticed, especially by Pharaoh's former cupbearer and baker. These men came to Joseph because they heard he might be able to help them understand the nightmares they had every night.

The cupbearer's dream was good news. He was about to be released from prison and appointed to his old position. Joseph told him the good news but pleaded, "When all goes well for you, remember that I was with you. Please show kindness to me by mentioning me to Pharaoh" (Genesis 40:14).

However once the chief cupbearer was released, he forgot all about Joseph.

Mr. Cupbearer returned to his prominent position and seemed to think nothing of Joseph during his two years of comfort. Conveniently, though, he had a sudden epiphany when Pharaoh's dreams proved traumatizing. Perhaps he hoped Pharaoh might give him a bounty for discovering Joseph. Whatever Mr. Cupbearer's motives, Joseph was called in to Pharaoh, and God gave Joseph the ability to interpret the dreams. Pharaoh was so impressed with Joseph that not only did he free him from prison, but he also granted Joseph power to rule equal only to Pharaoh.

Did you notice the cupbearer was more than happy to receive Joseph's good news when he was in need, but when his success and comforts returned, he forgot all about Joseph, the lowly prisoner?

Isn't this how we react sometimes with God? In trouble we expect God's immediate attention and action. Then a little comfort comes along, and our affections begin to shift, transitioning God to the background. But when you forget God, you forgo intimacy with Him.

Intimacy with God is conditional, just like intimacy in any other relationship. You cannot have a close connection to God if you only give Him access in certain situations. Intimacy with God means we are perpetually giving Him permission to participate in our lives. You share everything. You share your feelings, wants, desires, dreams, and disappointments.

You talk to Him, and He talks to you. Write Him a letter. Tell Him when:

- You're having feelings for that guy.
- You want a relationship but don't know if it's right.
- Your heart is confused, hurting, excited, in love, in like, etc.
- You feel alone or different.
- He noticed you.

Share your feelings with Jesus because He is Lord over all things, including our relationships. Not only that but He pursued us! He doesn't just want us to need Him; He wants us to want Him.

Will you be drawn to His kindness?

The Hard Work of Holiness

Not that I have already reached the goal or am already fully mature, but I make every effort to take hold of it because I also have been taken hold of by Christ Jesus. Brothers, I do not consider myself to have taken hold of it. But one thing I do: Forgetting what is behind and reaching forward to what is ahead, I pursue as my goal the prize promised by God's heavenly call in Christ Jesus.

—PHILIPPIANS 3:12–14

When I was a teenager, I spent Saturday afternoons falling asleep to the football games my grandfather watched. After marriage I spent Saturday afternoons falling asleep to the Clemson games my fanatical husband watched. Needless to say, I was in trouble when my husband's love for football lured my two sons into the sport.

I had no idea what to do when my five-year-old Jacob took the field for his first game. I watched passively for the first half, but something awakened in me during the second half. My body rose from my seat, and I found myself screaming: "Hit him! Hit him hard. You've got to hit him before he hits you!"

Shocked by this violent streak, I wished they had just chosen my sport: soccer. Here I am, a woman in ministry, yelling for my son not only to hit someone but to hit him *hard*.

I wasn't the only one entering a new world. The field I faced was full of boys ages five to eight. They had different levels of motivation and drive. Some worked hard while others rolled in the grass picking and blowing dandelions. The entire scene was comedic, but I tried to hide my smile when I saw the frustrated looks on their coaches' faces.

How do you keep a bunch of boys focused and motivated when they can hardly see past their enormous helmets?

One day it all changed. The boys were huddled in a circle, hands piled in the center chanting, "Hard work pays off!"

"What did you say?" the coach asked.

The blob shouted louder, "Hard work pays off!"

The idea wasn't original, but it was genius. Somehow he'd gotten a bunch of kids to preach to themselves and one another to work hard. The chant helped them focus, believe, and take responsibility for their actions, their game, and the outcome. Hard work, usually such a negative concept, had now become an essential motivator in their game.

Just like these boys, sometimes I feel distracted and scattered in my walk with God. My goal is to give God every area of my life, but often a dandelion comes along to distract me. Maybe you've dedicated your sexuality to God, but you find yourself distracted by a relationship, your feelings, your emotions, your friends, or maybe your doubt. When this happens, we need a little coaching.

Paul's words in Philippians 3:12–14 serve as a good "hard work pays off" chant for us. Paul had been beaten, betrayed, and put in prison for his faith, but before this he killed and persecuted Christians. His life constituted a long list of successes and failures, but he didn't focus on either. He worked hard to put all things behind him and focus instead on his prize. He understood that God deserved glory for each of his victories and that He had already saved him from all of his failures.

Sometimes we feel successful in our sexual purity, and sometimes we become disappointed in ourselves. The hard work pays off when we jump off the roller coaster and transition our vision and focus. We have to make the goal living and loving Jesus. When He is our focus, we will inevitably develop a spiritual intimacy that will undeniably produce the fruit of sexual purity in our lives.

pure by position

Create in me a pure heart, O God, and
renew a steadfast spirit within me.

—Psalm 51:10 NIV

Many of us have tried to fight for purity with our *performance*. Honestly, we've probably been taught that our performance determines how well we are doing spiritually so we make lists of what is holy, holier, and holiest. But this is not what Scripture teaches. Scripture appeals for us to fight for purity from our *position*. Let me explain.

We are drawn to a good performance. The better the performance, the more money it might make, the better the ratings. This may be a good entertainment principle, but if we apply the same principle to our fight for purity, one day we will find ourselves at the bottom of the barrel with no fight left in us. If you try harder and perform better, there is no guarantee that you will overcome your greatest struggle. Sometimes this principle pays off, but typically the harder we perform, the more discouraged we become when we mess up.

To successfully dedicate your sexuality to God, you must understand that **true purity comes from your position rather than your performance**. Purity doesn't come to you by trying harder or from your own human efforts. If you know Christ, your pure standing with God was given to you the day you received forgiveness and grace. You already possess a pure, holy, forgiven, and redeemed position because He paid for every one of your sins on the cross.

You are not fighting *for* a position of purity. You are fighting *from* a position of purity.

When Amber lost her virginity, shame and frustration kept her company for years because she knew she should have known better. She had a close relationship with God, but somehow her desire to be loved and belong to someone overpowered her will to save the gift of virginity for her wedding night. She didn't lose her relationship with God when she fell short of her goal, but she felt like she'd lost her right standing with God, and she wondered if she could earn back her purity.

Have you ever felt like you were wallowing in the bottom of a barrel with no hope of getting out? If you've ever been there, I'd like to encourage you with these words.

It is impossible for us to be perfect.

This is the reason Jesus died for each one of us. If you are His child, "He has given us a new birth into a living hope through the resurrection of Jesus Christ from the dead and into an inheritance that is imperishable, uncorrupted, and unfading, kept in heaven for you. You are being protected by God's power through faith for a salvation that is ready to be revealed in the last time. You rejoice in this, though now for a short time you have had to struggle in various trials" (1 Peter 1:3–6).

If you've fallen short or messed up, don't forget your *position*. Most often we forget who we are when we sin and try to make up for our incapabilities with good deeds of penance. But God wants you to remember that you are still His child. Your sin did not discredit the fact that you belong to Him. Remember your position as a child of God, repent, and determine again to live a life worthy of the calling you have received in Christ Jesus.

DAY
8

pure by practice

How can a young man
keep his way pure?
By keeping Your word.

—Psalm 119:9

I played on a basketball team that was second in the state two years in a row. I loved playing on this team because we were so good. But if you asked any player, she wouldn't claim to be the reason for our success. Our coach took us to state.

Our great weakness was free throws. Coach became sick of us missing shots from the foul line because they were missed opportunities, free points waiting to be counted. So he started a new tradition. Every day we were expected to make seven out of ten free throws. Every player (JV and varsity) had to run a "suicide" for every missed shot for every person who didn't make seven out of ten. Add it up.

None of us were happy with this new discipline. But our coach was smarter than we were. He knew that practice preceded performance. The way we performed during the game was a direct result of how we practiced.

If you want to win the game, you have to practice before you play. The way you play is a reflection of how you practice.

There's a lesson here for you in the area of purity and relationships. I talk to a lot of girls who want an amazing marriage and a loving husband, but they are making relationship choices now that contradict what they hope to have in the future. If you want to honor God with your body, with your relationships, and eventually with your marriage, you need to start practicing right now.

If you want a faithful marriage, you have to practice purity now. The person you are before your wedding day is the person you will be after. So many people assume a ring changes everything, but the two people who wear the rings determine the success of the marriage. Don't wait until you meet the man of your dreams or until you're engaged to practice purity. Start now.

Here are a few tips to get you started.

- Ask an older Christian woman to be your accountability partner. Your mom should be the first choice. If she isn't walking with God, ask a woman at your church or a youth worker. Be vulnerable with her about your struggles.
- Give God the first few moments of your day by reading Scripture and praying every morning before you go to school or work. It sets the tone for the rest of your day and places your mind on Christ, not desperate thoughts.

- Avoid movies, TV shows, and music that trigger feelings of loneliness or make you feel as if you *need* a guy to satisfy your loneliness.
- Decide now that you will not experiment sexually with a guy. Put it in writing and sign it. Give it to your parents, your pastor, or youth leader for accountability.
- If you struggle with lust, sign up for a free filtering service for your phone, tablet, and laptop that will make it extremely difficult to look at porn. Try Covenant Eyes or XXX Church.

Practice isn't always fun, but it's sure to help you win the game.

DAY 9

Pure by Participation

And let us be concerned about one another
in order to promote love and good works,
not staying away from our worship
meetings, as some habitually do, but
encouraging each other, and all the more
as you see the day drawing near.

—HEBREWS 10:24–25

When my son Joseph was seven years old, he decided to play football like his brother. But when I signed him up, they had a hard time finding enough players. They took the field for his first game with only eleven players. There were no subs and no room for sickness or injury. In my mind this team was sure to fail.

But something happened about halfway through the season. These five- to eight-year-olds learned to block, tackle, and run plays. The more the coach worked with them, the better they became. They started playing as a team, running touchdowns, and even ended up winning a game. My husband and I screamed and jumped up and down in celebration.

My son couldn't have won that game on his own against a team of eleven other players. He needed a team of guys around him to gain the victory.

The same thing is true in your battle to keep your sexuality within God's plan. Let me ask you a question: Why is it not unusual to find a group of girls gathered together talking about how dreamy or attractive a boy is, but it is much less familiar to hear them discussing whether said boy would be a godly or wise choice to date?

Let me answer my own question. Because our feelings, desires, and emotions run so deep, we'd rather go ahead and fulfill them and deal with our mistakes later than to have someone tell us now that we're headed in the wrong direction. It's not logical, but it's true.

However, when you became a Christian, you became part of a family, the church. Romans 7:4 says we "belong to another—to Him who was raised from the dead—that we may bear fruit for God." Living a life that glorifies God is a team effort, not an individual sport. If you try to win by yourself, you're guaranteeing your own defeat.

You're going to need people around you to help you win. People who will create a safe place for you to learn how to resist temptation, to confess your sin when you blow it, and to watch how older men and women love each other and treat each other. You need people in the church to teach and preach God's Word, to instruct and correct you so you don't walk into a bad decision.

Participating in church was integral in my fight for purity. I sat on the front row every Sunday and took notes when my pastor preached. I showed up early and stayed late whenever volunteers were needed. I learned that I belonged to a larger family that loved and cared for me and wanted me to become a woman of God. That reality made all the difference for me, and it can for you as well.

DAY 10

Pure by Planning

He stores up success for the upright;
He is a shield for those who live with
integrity so that He may guard
the paths of justice and protect the
way of His loyal followers.

—Proverbs 2:7–8

When I was a teenager, I became paranoid that I would lose my sight. My fear was unfounded and illogical, but it wouldn't go away. So I came up with a plan. I reasoned, "If I'm going to go blind, I've got to learn to take care of myself." One morning I refused to flip on the light switch and entered a pitch-black bathroom. I managed to wash my hair and body with no problems; unfortunately my legs suffered multiple razor wounds. After successfully dressing in the dark, I let myself cheat for hair and makeup. I didn't just do this for a day or a week but for months. Thankfully there is a little lesson from my obsession.

Your walk of purity may seem intimidating and unattainable, but I'm convinced most people give up because they didn't develop a plan. Without a plan you will fall flat on your face every time sin knocks on your door. Temptation wants to devour and fill your life with regret and shame so you need to be prepared. Take a look at today's verses from Proverbs again. A solid plan devised ahead of time is better than a desperate prayer in the heat of the moment. So I wanted to give you a simple plan made of three simple phrases:

1. Hate it. One of the reasons we choose to sin is because we secretly believe it is a source of happiness instead of harm. Fish are continually hooked because the enticing and yummy worm disguises the deadly hook lurking inside. When you are tempted, you have to choose to remember the destruction your sinful choices have created in the past. You have to start loving Jesus more than your sin. Don't take the bait. Choose to hate!

2. Starve it. The power of sexual sin grows stronger the more you feed it. If you're constantly absorbing relationship tips from magazines, television shows, the Internet, or your friends, how do you ever expect to understand or adopt godly ideals? It's hard to dedicate your sexuality to God if you're addicted to looking at porn or having a physical relationship with your boyfriend. You have to replace the bad habits with better ones. Join a small group or start listening to sermons daily on iTunes. Starve the sin by feeding your spirit.

3. Outsmart it. Outsmarting sin means you think of ways to preempt the pressure to sin. Here are some practical steps:

- Stay away from situations where you would be alone with a boy in the dark.

- Set a curfew with your parents so you don't find yourself too tired to make a godly decision.
- Commit to sexual abstinence until marriage and allow an older sister in Christ to give you dating advice.
- Don't hide relationships from your parents.
- Don't follow people on Twitter or be friends with people on Facebook who post images or links that will take you to tempting pages or images.

Many of us pray prayers and make promises only to become disappointed when they don't work out. But how many of us made these heartfelt commitments without considering the action our words required? It's not bad to promise and pray, but it's better to follow up those intentions with a plan of action.

How will you plan to protect yourself from sin?

pure in perspective

A thief comes only to steal and to kill and to destroy. I have come so that they may have life and have it in abundance.

—JOHN 10:10

Satan's goal is to use your sin to make you feel separated from the love of God. Let me show you how he tricks us all.

1. If you have a past full of regrets and mistakes . . .

- He lies to you and tells you that you have to earn God's favor, but at the same time he tells you that you will never be able to do it.
- He tells you that you might as well give up and give in to sin because you'll never succeed in anything holy or righteous.
- He tells you that you'll never be able to change so you decide to live it up, hoping God will cover it up later when it's time to pay up.
- He uses your feelings of inadequacy to keep you from knowing God's unconditional love and acceptance.

2. If you've lived a (comparatively) mild life of sin . . .

- He tries to find whatever glaring sin you are trying to hide.

- He pinpoints your weak spot, hammering you with condemnation until you feel unworthy and useless to God.
- He tells you to give up or to begin working your fingers to the bone to make up for your inadequacies.
- He uses your feelings of shame to keep you from knowing God's unconditional grace and acceptance.

Satan is no fool. He has been using the same lies on God's children for generations. Sadly we often absorb his lies into our emotions. They feel so familiar to us that they have become part of our theology on who God is. The enemy will do anything to keep us from a healthy relationship with God.

But God has also been speaking a message to His children for generations. His message to you is much more encouraging so open up your heart and get ready.

1. "That is, in Christ, God was reconciling the world to Himself, not counting their trespasses against them, and He has committed the message of reconciliation to us" (2 Corinthians 5:19). God sent Jesus to pay for all the pain of your sins

because His heart is not to punish you. This is and always has been His heart for you and anyone else who chooses to believe.

2. "Therefore, if anyone is in Christ, he is a new creation; old things have passed away, and look, new things have come" (2 Corinthians 5:17). God see you as a brand-new person. So leave the regret of your past mistakes behind and start pursuing the new person He is creating inside.

3. "Do not remember the past events, pay no attention to things of old. Look, I am about to do something new; even now it is coming. Do you not see it? Indeed, I will make a way in the wilderness, rivers in the desert" (Isaiah 43:18–19). Stop looking at your past and trying to make it better. One day all the things you can't bear will become beautiful. He's already started the process so put hope in what He's already healed and move forward.

Stop listening to Satan's negative lies, and tune your ear to the truths of God's Word. Let His words draw you closer to Him and the future He has waiting for you.

Appetite

For the grace of God has appeared
with salvation for all people, instructing
us to deny godlessness and worldly
lusts and to live in a sensible, righteous,
and godly way in the present age.

—Titus 2:11–12

Many Christians assume their appetite for sex is sinful or something they should be ashamed of. This is not true. Your sexual appetite and attraction for a guy is not naturally evil. In fact, God made you with the desire to experience and enjoy intimate love. But in His design the experience is to be shared with your husband.

Here are a few reasons God gave us the gift of sex:

1. Procreation. Sex is the physical act that leads to children. For human life to continue and our species to avoid extinction, babies have to be born. In order for babies to be born, babies have to be made. You get the point.

2. Recreation. Sex is fun. It feels good. It's an enjoyable activity that should be mutually experienced by a man and woman within the covenant of marriage. It's so good, as a matter of fact, that married people actually keep doing it after the honeymoon. For decades. OK, enough about that.

3. Communication. Sexual intimacy is built on mutual trust between a husband and a wife. It's a means of communicating that trust, as well as the love and respect and affection the two spouses feel for each other. The two bodies act and respond to each other, communicating deep commitment and vulnerability.

If you are like I was at your age, you're reading this and saying, "OK, I get it, but if God gave me a hunger to be satisfied sexually, why do I have to wait so long to enjoy it? What is the purpose of this in-between time?"

Like all appetites, having a desire doesn't mean you need immediate fulfillment. Sometimes an appetite must be controlled because an appetite without limits is destructive.

God uses the "in-between" time to teach us much needed self-control. Yep, I said "self-control," that dreaded, anti-American word. We hate this word because we live in a world where we see, we want, we click, we buy, and it's delivered. Instant gratification. The idea that we have to wait more than three to five days for delivery is foreign. So to even suggest that God might have us wait *years* to satisfy a physical desire feels like sheer torture.

Self-control is a gift to your relationships in that the amount of self-control you learn before marriage translates into your marriage later on. If your boyfriend or you are unable to control your sexual desires now, who's to say you won't tire of being faithful in marriage? Walking down an aisle doesn't make someone faithful and self-controlled. But if you can repeatedly lean on the grace of God to teach you self-control, you will see later on what a gift it was to suffer through your trial for a while in order to have a decades-long marriage and family built on trust and faithful love.

DAY 13

Insecurities

The LORD is faithful in all His
words and gracious in all His actions.

—PSALM 145:13

Have you ever watched a chain smoker? First, she'll pop the box against her hand until one lucky cigarette peeps out of the bottom. Two fingers bring the cigarette up to her mouth while, simultaneously, the other hand reaches for the lighter. She flicks the wheel, inhales the red flames into the end of the cigarette, and a puff comes out of her mouth. In only a few minutes, the cigarette has burned to the nub.

And before the nub is fully extinguished in one hand, the other hand already has the box of new smokes ready. It's time to repeat the process.

Sometimes I sit and listen to girls talk about the long list of boys who have never given them what they need. Each breakup leaves them dissatisfied and disillusioned. They don't know who they are, what they like, or whom they want to be.

And before their hearts are healed, their eyes are already looking for the next guy who will change it all.

It's time to repeat the process.

Chain dating is as destructive as chain smoking. Sure, smoking can kill your body, but chain dating creates a chasm of insecurity in your soul as it eats away your identity.

If chain dating makes people miserable, what makes it so addictive? You were originally designed to find absolute fulfillment in your relationship with God, but that fellowship was messed up in the garden of Eden. The passion you have to find love and security is designed primarily to lead you to a relationship with Jesus and secondarily to share life with your husband. Unfortunately in our impatience we try to fill the emptiness in our hearts with one guy after another.

Some of my worst relationship decisions were made on the rebound, out of insecurity. I didn't give my hurting heart time to heal from the last guy before I picked up the next. Boom! Suddenly a new guy in shining armor came along to distract me before I could realize the danger of my addiction.

Chain dating originates from a need to find something other than God to fill our needs. So it only makes sense that nothing other than the presence of God can defeat the effects of this addiction in our lives. We have to stop looking for a guy to satisfy us and start backing up our faith with action.

I know it will take faith to believe He really sees you and loves you. I know it will take trust to believe He will satisfy you. But here is my challenge: Take a break from guys for a while. Watch God meet your needs. I'm not saying it will be easy, but every girl I know who has done this and stuck with it has become more secure and confident in herself and in her relationship with God. I know this will be true for you.

DAY 14

Comparisons

Run from sexual immorality! "Every
sin a person can commit is outside the
body." On the contrary, the person who is
sexually immoral sins against his own
body. Don't you know that your body is
a sanctuary of the Holy Spirit who is in
you, whom you have from God? You are
not your own, for you were bought at a
price. Therefore glorify God in your body.

—1 Corinthians 6:18–20

When my friend Sarah confessed her secret sexual sins to her friends, they replied with a list of comparisons:

"I've let a guy touch me, but I didn't have sex."

"I've kissed a guy, and we took our shirts off, but we didn't get naked."

"I've done this and that but definitely NOT THAT."

"Wow, I'm glad I didn't go as far as you."

When she was telling me about their conversation, she told me she realized that each girl had created her own list of what were acceptable and unacceptable forms of intimacy. But the standards were not all the same. In fact, many times standards changed according to "how far" they'd gone with their last boyfriend.

A lot of Christian young women ask me, "How far is too far?"

Some of them want a solid answer so they can draw a line in the sand, a protective barrier to keep sin far away. Others are hoping my answer will be vague so they can satisfy their sexual desires without truly crossing the line. For example, if I were to say, "Don't have sex before marriage," they'd participate in a variety of intimate pleasures with their boyfriend without actually going "all the way."

But the goal in dedicating your sexuality is to avoid both legalism and abusive grace. To do this you have to let go of your comparisons. Forget "the list." Don't compare your actions to your girlfriends. Don't let your boyfriend dictate your intimacy standards. If you're truly allowing the gospel to define your purity, the most important person to consider is God.

How you treat your body is not about what your friend does with her body or what your boyfriend wants you to do with your body. How you treat your body is about what you believe about your body. When you became a Christian, God decided that your body was the perfect place for Him to live. You became a temple, a place for the Holy Spirit to occupy.

So let me ask you a question: "How far is too far?"

- **How far is too far** for you to go in dedicating your body and your sexuality to a God who died to give you life?
- **How far is too far** for you to start seeing your sexuality as part of your testimony, part of the gospel story in your life?

- **How far is too far** to stop comparing your sexual behavior with the actions of your friends and instead start dedicating your behavior to the God who lives inside you?

It's up to you. Will you let go of your lists?

DAY 15

Flirt

Discretion will watch over you,
and understanding will guard you,
rescuing you from the way of evil.

—Proverbs 2:11–12

Clayton and I were doing a Q&A on stage when these words of wisdom flowed from my husband's mouth.

"What you win them with is what you win them *to*."

Wow, I thought, *I must have taught him that.* (Just kidding.)

Clayton is the greatest gift God has brought into my life. He embarrasses me on a regular basis with exaggerated proclamations of my matchless beauty. While I'm glad he hasn't yet broken the spell I put over him, I'm completely aware that he could have chosen many other beautiful women. But I'm glad he picked me and remains my biggest admirer.

We spent a lot of time apart when we were dating because he traveled to preach four days a week or more. Because I spent most of my days in our little town, I developed a fear that he would discover a new gem to love on a faraway adventure. I waited for the devastating day that he'd reveal his newfound love during a dinner date. I lived in fear.

Fear is our biggest enemy. It lies and deceives us into making bad decisions. Fear tried to convince me that I needed to do something to "keep"

Clayton around. For females the most predominant lie is that sexual intimacy keeps a boy interested. Thankfully God helped me fight the lies. We didn't have sex before we were married, and we've been married since May 1999.

But what Clayton said is true. "What you win them with is what you win them to." If you catch a guy with sensual flirting or keep a trap with sexual favors, this is what you've won him to. You've captured his lust, not his love. If he is put off because you're not "putting out," sex is all he really wants.

I know this is hard to hear and even harder to live out. A close friend of mine once told me that even Christian guys expect sex, and if you don't compromise, they'll just find someone who will. But let me ask you two questions:

- How long before he becomes uninterested in your intimate interaction?
- How long before another girl's advances catch his attention?

If you catch a guy on the premise of sexual satisfaction, you are flirting with disaster.

God wants to give you a man who loves you for you, not your body. But He can't accomplish this if you choose to make unwise choices. "Pay careful attention, then, to how you walk—not as unwise people but as wise" (Ephesians 5:15). Your goal should be to make choices from a place of wisdom, not worry. In wisdom you trust God to provide a good man when you are ready. In worry you may catch him with sensual flirting, but when the physical pleasure dies, so will the relationship.

So next time you feel the flirt coming on, go back and read today's proverb.

DAY 16

Fall

You pushed me hard to make
me fall, but the LORD helped me.
The LORD is my strength and my song;
He has become my salvation.

—PSALM 118:13–14

We all fall. You may feel alone in your failure, but you're not. Each Christian has selfish cravings, which try to override our call to righteousness. Our souls swing on a pendulum of struggle between serving ourselves and surrendering to God.

The apostle Paul struggled with sin too. He said, "I do not understand what I am doing, because I do not practice what I want to do, but I do what I hate. . . . When I want to do what is good, evil is with me. For in my inner self I joyfully agree with God's law. But I see a different law in the parts of my body, waging war against the law of my mind and taking me prisoner to the law of sin in the parts of my body. What a wretched man I am! Who will rescue me from this dying body? I thank God through Jesus Christ our Lord!" (Romans 7:15, 21–25).

One of our biggest temptations is to trust ourselves more than God. If we give in to this temptation, we deceive ourselves into believing that our thoughts, desires, and feelings are truer than God's. This is self-worship. We must be aware when self-worship tries to enter our hearts because it is what corrupted Satan. His "heart became proud because of [his] beauty; for the sake of [his] splendor [he] corrupted [his] wisdom" (Ezekiel 28:17).

When you are struggling with sexual temptation, self-worship whispers, "You deserve a life filled with pleasure. Don't deny yourself anything, including boys, romance, or sex. If you want it, go ahead and take it. Your desires are meant to be satisfied."

It's hard to recognize the voice trying to lure us away from trusting God because self-worship has become commonplace in our culture. Media advertisements don't propagate self-control but rather self-satisfaction. They preach, "Give in to your urges, and feed them. Get what you want; take what you need." And the more money they make off of you, the louder their broadcast becomes.

But God doesn't see you as a commodity.

He wants you to experience an abundant life, full of peace and satisfaction, but you will never acquire this by serving yourself. John the Baptist explained this principle in his confession, "He must increase, but I must decrease" (John 3:30). Spiritual security and satisfaction only come when we keep selfishness at bay by giving Jesus the highest place in our lives.

One activity I've adopted from Beth Moore's book *Jesus: 90 Days with the One and Only* is to pray for God to help me recognize when my "selves" are getting in the way of the Holy Spirit. I pray for Him to help me keep these "selves" under control:

- self-exaltation
- self-protection
- self-righteousness
- self-will
- self-loathing
- self-worship
- self-serving
- self-promotion
- self-indulgence
- self-absorption
- self-delusion
- self-pity
- self-sufficiency

If we want to keep from falling, we must first recognize and repent from our tendency to be self-worshipers. Second, we have to keep placing Jesus in the most prominent place of our hearts. And finally, we must pray for our "selves," that we will submit them to God's rule in humility.

Voluntary Forgiveness

If we confess our sins, He is faithful and righteous to forgive us our sins and to cleanse us from all unrighteousness.

—1 John 1:9

Nothing feels worse than disappointing God, yourself, your parents, your future husband, your friends, or pretty much anyone who expected you to be the Christian you portrayed yourself to be. You love Jesus, and you want Him to know how much you love Him, too, but you messed up. And somehow messing up in our sexual lives feels so much more disappointing than other sins.

Lying, cheating, stealing, getting drunk, gossiping, jealousy, hate, and so many other sins seem easier to explain away or justify. You know they aren't right, but the consequences don't feel so dirty and degrading. It's much harder to forgive yourself for sexual sin. And even more than that, the biggest hurdle I've ever encountered is believing God watched me sin and will still forgive. Open up your heart, and let me assure you that not only does He want to forgive you but He already has.

A young man was sick of his father. He told his father he wished he were dead so he could inherit his fortune. The father was insulted and hurt, but he did not retaliate. He handed over the inheritance and watched his son walk away.

Years later the son had nothing left to show for his life. He had nowhere to live, nowhere to work, and no food to eat. In his desperation he remembered his father's employees were paid more than he'd received in months. A last-ditch effort led him home to beg for a job.

When I read the story of the prodigal son in Luke 15, every prophetic cell in my body knows the father possesses the right to turn his son away, to offer a silencing hand to any disrespectful word his son might offer.

The situation screamed for justice, punishment, and rejection, but a call to grace captivated this father's heart. *This father* met his son with compassionate arms and a house full of food and favor.

When his son arrived, this father did not stare into the son's eyes with an attitude of debate or conflict. He did not hesitate, wondering if his son's plea would make up for all the disgrace. No, the son was immediately met with forgiveness because the father had forgiven the son when he was still far away. The son was forgiven before he even reached his father's doorstep, not because he deserved it but because the father loved him so much.

This is the Father you come to when you need forgiveness. He waits with arms of compassion and a heart of favor. His greatest desire is to love you and spend time with you. Do you believe it? Can you receive it? He is waiting.

Protective Forgiveness

All of us have become like something
unclean, and all our righteous acts
are like a polluted garment; all of
us wither like a leaf, and our iniquities
carry us away like the wind.

—Isaiah 64:6

The principles of Scripture are true. They are designed to bring life to our hurting hearts, but sometimes it takes years for our emotions to absorb the truths our souls recognize.

Here is one truth that has taken me years to feel: God forgave me to set me free, not to make me feel ashamed and guilty.

Do you believe this? I don't mean in your mind; I mean in your gut. When you stand before God with all your sin and shortcomings, do you believe God wants to punish or protect you?

When the prodigal son made his way home, he knew the disrespectful way he had treated his father years before was punishable by death. Not only did the letter of the law give the father permission to kill his son, but any other family member or employee was also justified for such action.

As Christians, our souls know that God has every right to demand our lives from us, to punish us for falling short. In our pride sometimes we may wish for punishment above exemption. But this is not the heart of our Father.

The prodigal's father *ran* to his son. This may have been out of fondness and excitement, but another motivation might have been his urgency to save his son's life. He rushed out to see his son and placed his own robe around his son's shoulders, a symbol of acceptance and protection. Perhaps his speed to meet his son was motivated by the fear that someone less forgiving might take his son's life before he could cover him with a robe of protection.

Sin carries with it a sense of scorn, but Jesus died to remove this plague from our lives. When we sin, instead of accepting forgiveness as a badge of shame, God wants to clothe us in robes of redemption and protection. I have reiterated the fact that we are incapable of perfection. God knows it. You know it. I know it.

So throw off your filthy rags. Forgiveness serves as your protection in two ways.

First, it disarms anyone who may point out your flaws by acknowledging you are incapable of accomplishing what Christ did on the cross. Instead you rest in His ability to make things right.

Second, it cleanses your conscience before God. Hebrews 9:14 asks, "How much more will the blood of the Messiah, who through the eternal Spirit offered Himself without blemish to God, cleanse our consciences from dead works to serve the living God?" In other words, if Jesus' blood was able to pay the infinite debt of sin and present Him faultless before God, surely His blood will do that for you as well! When your soul's emotions are able to grasp this truth, then you can move forward and serve God.

God doesn't want you to waste any more time wondering about your punishment. He died for your freedom.

Fellowship

For God did not appoint us to wrath,
but to obtain salvation through our Lord
Jesus Christ, who died for us, so that
whether we are awake or asleep, we
will live together with Him. Therefore
encourage one another and build each
other up as you are already doing.

—1 THESSALONIANS 5:9–10

The word *fellowship* has the ability to foster hope and affection or fear and rejection. We were made to crave true fellowship, but often we hold others at arm's length, wondering if we will be accepted for who we are. Will our risk be met with promise or lead us into a world of betrayal and hurt? Do faithful friends exist? And if they do, do we deserve any?

We all know incorrect fellowship can damage and disappoint our souls, but this reality will never eliminate our God-infused drive to share love and life with others. So, what's a girl to do? We have to start changing the way we do friendships. If we're willing to become good "fellowshippers," we usher in the power of hope-filled, healing relationships into our lives.

My friend Sarah's story, that I mentioned earlier, is a perfect example of this. We were standing at the island in her kitchen when she opened her soul to me. She had started dating in high school, and in an unexpected, vulnerable moment, she gave her boyfriend her sexuality for the first time. A few boyfriends later she was sick in her sin. So she desperately tried to realign her faith in God with her actions, but changing her habits proved harder than she thought.

So Sarah gathered a few Christian friends whom she thought would push her forward in her pursuit of purity. After confessing everything, she sat in front of them, wounded. Her friends encouraged her with the words:

Friend 1: "Well, I've let a guy touch me, but I didn't have sex."

Friend 2: "I've kissed a guy, and we took our shirts off, but we didn't get naked."

Friend 3: "I've done this and that, but definitely NOT THAT."

Friend 4: "Wow, I'm glad I didn't go as far as you."

She sat there. Stunned. Their words pinned her down like poisonous darts filled with condemnation and comparison. Their careless comments hit the bull's-eye in her crippled heart, and her trust came crumbling down.

I don't think Sarah's friends meant to be vindictive or malicious, but they were careless. Have you ever noticed that a sincere desire to encourage sometimes morphs as it travels from your mind and comes out of your mouth? I've been there and done that. So God showed me today's passage from 1 Thessalonians.

God wants us to encourage one another because He never wanted us to have to live a life struggling with sin but full of life. And since we aren't yet living in heaven with Him, He wants us to help one another out in this world, speaking words of life and encouragement instead of discouragement and death.

So, when you are trying to encourage a friend, ask yourself, *Are the words I'm about to say giving her hope, or are my words full of death and condemnation?* If what you want to say isn't promoting the victory Christ gives us against our sin, wait before you speak. Listen a little bit longer. Wait until God gives you the proper encouragement for the situation.

If you are willing to check your heart, hold your tongue, and listen before you speak, you will become a better "fellowshipper." When you improve your ability to fellowship, you will find truer, lasting friendships.

Fight

But thanks be to God, who gives us the
victory through our Lord Jesus Christ!

—1 CORINTHIANS 15:57

The flesh and blood you see is like a dream. Don't let your mind play tricks that lead to fear and rage. See light. Be light. I am with you always. Always.

—Ted Dekker, *Sovereign*

I'm not really into boxing, but I watched the Tyson versus Holyfield match in 1997 with a group of college friends. I tried to keep my eyes open, but the fighting made me cringe, block my face with my hands, and scream, "Do something!" I learned I can't stand watching someone get incessantly pummeled.

How do you feel in your battle against sin? Maybe sometimes you're able to keep your gloves up or land a punch. But how often do you feel alone, crouch in the corner of the ring, and slink down, hopeless? In your moment of desperation, I wish you could see in the spirit realm. I believe all of heaven would be on their feet, cheering and screaming, "Do something!"

I recently watched a movie called *Real Steel* (a robot-boxing movie) with my boys. The son had been trying to capture his father's attention, but the father continually made the son feel abandoned and unimportant. Exasperated, the father finally asked his son, "What do you want from me?"

The son responded: "I want you to fight for me. That's all I've ever wanted."

When you're stuck in the corner, you want someone to fight for you. Your battle with temptation has left you weary, tired, and defeated. You're hoping for a fresh cup of compassion. When you're down on the bottom, you can give up and lose, or you can take confidence in the fact that Jesus has already won your battle.

You wanted someone to fight for you, right? Jesus did. He defeated sin and death on the cross. He wants you to be victorious against sin, but you have to fight a little differently than you are now.

Don't fight *for* victory but *from* victory.

Here's how it works.

When feelings of loneliness, depression, passion, or lust corner you, when your mind is desperate and your emotions don't have the energy to fight any longer, remember Christ overcame everything you're up against. As Romans 8:11 tells us, "And if the Spirit of Him who raised Jesus from the dead lives in you, then He who raised Christ from the dead will also bring your mortal bodies to life through His Spirit who lives in you."

You fight from victory when:

- You realize Jesus has already overcome your sin (Romans 8:35–39).
- You understand that God placed the Holy Spirit, who raised Christ from the dead, inside you (Romans 8:11–14).
- You allow the Holy Spirit to transform you and strengthen you to fight sin by focusing your thoughts away from your feelings and toward Jesus (Romans 13:14).
- You learn to hate the effects of sin in your life (Romans 12:9).
- You realize that sin killed Christ, but God's life-giving power raised Him from death (Romans 6:10–11).
- You understand that sin may be enticing, but it is not life-giving (Romans 6:23).

In your fight for purity, don't forget: you are not alone. God is fighting for you. You don't fight *for* victory but *from* victory. I believe the God who lives in you will bring you to victory. Keep fighting.

Flee

Flee from youthful passions,
and pursue righteousness, faith,
love, and peace, along with those who
call on the Lord from a pure heart.

—2 Timothy 2:22

The best way to fight sin is to flee temptation.

It was Friday night. I was tired of not being invited to the "fun" parties. My new friend was interested in a guy who invited her to a party. I agreed to drive since I wouldn't be drinking.

When we arrived, I knew this was not the place for me. I was sitting alone at a stranger's kitchen table when a guy sat down and invited me to a back bedroom. I snapped out of my lethargy, walked into the living room, and told her it was time to go. I couldn't take any more.

I didn't realize it then, but that's exactly what Paul had written to his disciple Timothy in the Scripture above.

1. Run from evil. Temptation always grabs us at the heart level, promising us something that we crave or desire, but these promises come up empty after a while. So how do you know what is evil? If you pay close attention, when you are coming close to an unwise decision or a tempting situation, the Holy Spirit will warn your soul to run, to flee, to say no to any ungodly situation. Our job is to stay aware, listen, and run.

2. Stay close to righteousness. As you are running away from evil, don't stop until you know

FOR GIRLS

you've started running toward Christ. Jesus influences our desires to want what is right. Are you spending time with Him, allowing Him to create a clean heart, one that seeks righteousness? You cannot flee temptation without focusing on Jesus.

3. Find a fellowship. Sometimes you may feel sad or lonely as you walk away from sin. Find a companion for these lonely times. But be careful whom you choose. Not everyone will encourage you on your path to purity. You are searching for someone who will support you in your walk with Christ, who will stand with you on your journey of sexual purity.

Although I escaped a bad situation by the skin of my chinny-chin-chin, I didn't make a wise decision to go to this party to begin with. I let my insecurity, my desire to win my friends' approval, put me in a bad situation. I should have run and headed in the other direction. I shouldn't have looked, considered, or flirted with the idea of going.

Flee! This strategy is effective because you are not strong enough to fight sexual sin and temptation in your own power. But remember that the power that raised Jesus Christ from the dead lives

87

within you. He is ready to help you run, stay close, and find a friend.

DAY 22

Refuse

Therefore, submit to God. But resist the
Devil, and he will flee from you.

—JAMES 4:7

My natural attraction to him was irresistible. He was pleasant to the eyes, and I liked that little feeling in my stomach when I was around him. It seemed like he came alive in my presence too. I knew I was in trouble. My heart was hooked, but my spirit screamed sounds of warning. Danger.

Butterflies of excitement fluttered when the professor paired us together for a class assignment. We worked together each week, and soon he kept me up-to-date on his social life. Each Friday opened new opportunities to find a new party and a new girl or perhaps a few new girls.

I listened, knowing it was a mistake to entertain any kind of future relationship because we were different in every way. But I'd catch myself walking across campus imagining myself with him, formulating wishful scenarios in which a relationship could work. Even though I knew it could never work, my feelings relentlessly fought my soul to get their way.

Class let out, and we took the sidewalk to the other side of campus. Then the moment of decision came. Looking at each other, he asked me to date him. This was the first time a college guy had asked me out, but all I felt was conflict.

I'm sure the battle between my emotions and my spirit was evident. I could hardly look into his eyes because I was afraid they'd steal away my courage to make the wise decision. I was wrapped in a blanket of disappointment and excitement.

I knew I could say yes, but this meant I'd be breaking my word and three of my commitments to God. First, I would be dating a guy who had no relationship with God. Second, I made a decision not to date my freshman year so I could focus on finding friends who would encourage me in my relationship with God. Not only would a relationship with this guy break my commitment to God, but it would also steal time away from new friendships. Third, a relationship with this guy meant compromise in my sexual purity. He saw girls as a commodity, a form of entertainment. I knew he was a charmer, but I wanted to believe the little lies floating through my heart tricking me into thinking he'd treat me better than "all the other girls." But in truth He would be too interested in self-gratification to protect my purity.

The choice I had that day on the sidewalk is the same choice you will face in your sexuality decisions. The situation may be different, but the heart issue is the same: whom will we choose and whom will we refuse?

Ephesians 5:3, 6–8 tells us clearly, "But sexual immorality and any impurity or greed should not even be heard of among you, as is proper for saints. . . . Let no one deceive you with empty arguments. . . . Therefore, do not become their partners. For you were once darkness, but now you are light in the Lord. Walk as children of light."

Here's the raw truth. Success in your sexual purity depends on whom you choose to refuse. God will help us live as His children, dedicating our sexuality to Him and protecting us from being deceived into making bad choices. But our job is to listen, to learn, and to refuse the bad choices that often tempt us.

I said no to the guy on the sidewalk, but it wasn't easy. I wasn't tempted by his lifestyle, but a part of me yearned for his affection and attention. Still I knew that if I compromised in my decision to date him, soon it wouldn't be so hard to earn his affection through satisfying him physically. I was uncomfortable rejecting him, but I was even more disturbed at the idea of breaking my promise to Jesus.

Whom will you chose to refuse?

DAY 23

reject

I will be a Father to you,
and you will be sons and daughters
to Me, says the Lord Almighty.

—2 CORINTHIANS 6:18

My date drove me home from prom and walked me to the door. In my mind I was already trying to think of a way of getting out of the kiss.

I walked fast so I could squeeze my body inside the storm door. Ugh, the back door was locked. I could feel his presence standing on the step right behind me.

He's gonna try anyway, I thought.

So I whipped out my key and looked in the window.

"I think I see my mom," I said. The house was pitch black. My mom was probably in bed, but I didn't want a kiss!

With a quick turn of my key, the door unlocked.

I scooted inside, leaving a crack to say, "Goodbye." And I slunk down the wall in the hall. I breathed a sigh of relief and guilt in one long exhale.

You might be saying, "Sharie, it was only a kiss." You're right. But I was crystal clear when I agreed to go to prom with him *as friends*. I meant it. I didn't want to get involved beyond a friendship. But his feelings created expectations, which made me feel obligated to "give" him something.

When you go on a date, to a movie, to eat, or to a game, you don't owe anyone anything. You don't owe them anything for money spent. You don't owe them anything because you had fun or because they like you or think you are pretty.

Your body was created and given to you by your Father, the King of heaven. You don't owe any part of yourself to anyone because you feel guilty or because they expect it. In fact, you have every right to reject it.

But sometimes we feel guilty for leaving someone's heart on our doorstep. So here are some verses to help you reject what is not right for you.

1. "But to all who did receive Him, He gave them the right to be children of God, to those who believe in His name, who were born, not of blood, or of the will of the flesh, or of the will of man, but of God" (John 1:12–13).
2. "Finally then, brothers, we ask and encourage you in the Lord Jesus, that as you have received from us how you must walk and please God—as you are doing—do so even more" (1 Thessalonians 4:1).
3. "Yet the righteous person will hold to his way, and the one whose hands are clean will grow stronger" (Job 17:9).

I wasn't comfortable kissing this guy, but that didn't stop him from trying. When you find yourself in this situation, remember the lessons from these verses.

1. You are God's daughter. You have the right to live your life the way He has called you.
2. Because you are a daughter of the King of heaven, you are primarily supposed to please Him. If that doesn't please the guy you're with, he can find someone else.
3. Every time you make a decision for purity, you will become stronger as the gospel defines who you are in your sexuality.

While rejecting what is not right for you may feel awkward at times—like the comical end to my prom date—it helps you accept the perfect promise of God. And that promise will last *for all time.*

DAY 24

Redirect

He will also strengthen you to the end, so
that you will be blameless in the day of
our Lord Jesus Christ. God is faithful; you
were called by Him into fellowship with
His Son, Jesus Christ our Lord.

—1 CORINTHIANS 1:8–9

40 DAYS OF PURITY

Have you ever been fishing? When I was a little girl, I fished in my grandparents' pond. I noticed that the fishing line often looked bent under the water. I later learned that this is because water bends light as it travels through.

Archerfish eat insects that hover above the water. Since water bends light, God designed them with the natural tendency to redirect the angle at which they hunt. "The archer fish swims beneath its prey so that its line of sight is true. It then spits a jet of water, knocking the unlucky insect off its perch. Then, it's lunchtime."[1] Although the science of water and light may seem to work against the archerfish, God equipped the fish with exactly what it needed to survive.

Many girls pursue sexual purity from the wrong angle, looking through the water, focusing on virginity alone. But virginity alone cannot be our ultimate goal because it has the capacity for failure. Like the archerfish, we have to redirect our focus. The ultimate goal isn't to be a virgin on your wedding day but to belong to Jesus on judgment day.

Right now you might be thinking, *But, Sharie isn't that the purpose of this book—to help me be a virgin on my wedding day?*

Yes, of course, I want that for you. But virginity alone, while a good goal, cannot be your ultimate goal because it can fail you. Think about it this way: obedience to a regulation doesn't carry the same weight as obedience to your ruler, Jesus Christ. Virginity is a by-product of our love and passion for Christ, not the opposite.

Many Christian girls believe their sexual status is congruent with their status in Christ. They believe virginity makes Jesus love them more. Confused females approach me asking, "I've _____. Am I still a virgin?" "This happened to me when I was a little girl. Am I still a virgin?" "My boyfriend_____. Am I still a virgin?" Rules and guilt have brought them to a place of fear. What they're really asking is, "I can't change my past. Does Jesus still love me?"

If this is you, you need to redirect your focus. Our motivation for purity must originate with the One who made you in love. You cannot let fear and guilt manipulate your sexuality because they will leave you feeling confused and defeated. Jesus' love and compassion must guide your sexual journey so that you have someone to bring you back if you stray.

Let this verse give you strength: "I lift my eyes toward the mountains. Where will my help come from? My help comes from the LORD, the Maker of heaven and earth" (Psalm 121:1–2).

Virginity is a thing, a standard, a regulation. It doesn't have the capacity to produce holiness or right standing in your life with God. If we are defining our sexuality with the gospel, we cannot make virginity an idol. Rather, we worship Jesus and let fellowship with Him give us victory over sexual temptation.

Redefine

"I am the bread of life," Jesus told them.
"No one who comes to Me will ever be
hungry, and no one who believes in Me
will ever be thirsty again."

—JOHN 6:35

In the summer of 1999, my husband and I led a medical mission trip to the Himalayas. For three weeks we backpacked two hundred miles into remote villages with a thirty-eight-year-old single doctor named Anna. For years Dr. Anna had led medical mission trips during her vacations, but just before our trip she decided to sell everything, leave her hospital job in the States, and move to India.

It seemed like Anna had given up so much already. How could she keep on giving things up and remain satisfied?

Sitting by the campfire one night, Anna told us about her encounter with her hero, Mother Teresa. Anna hopped on a train one day bound for Calcutta. When she arrived at the hospital, one of the nuns escorted her to the back of a tent where a small-framed woman was bent over her patient. It was Mother Teresa.

Anna stood to the side, watching as Mother Teresa stared into a leprous man's face with kind eyes, singing over him. A pail sitting at her feet kept making an awkward clinking sound. Anna soon noticed her sweet sister was using her fragile fingers to remove maggots from the man's face and then drop them into the pail. The man's condition was terminal, and he did not have long to live. Still, Mother Teresa considered him worthy of her love and comfort.

Tear-filled, Anna walked out refusing to interrupt this moment. As I was listening and looking into the campfire, my eyes too filled with tears. I sat there thinking about these two amazing women.

Mother Teresa had no husband, family, money, or home. She had love for Jesus and a love for people. She was happy. Dr. Anna gave up her country, her home, and her career to serve in India for a lifetime. She is content.

One of the scariest areas we have to give to God is our physical desire, our sexuality. Before I was married, I wondered what I might be missing and whether it would be worth it in the end. Maybe you've shared the same thoughts as me, like: *Why does everyone else get to enjoy sex and not me? Doesn't God want me to experience love fully? Why is He keeping sex from me?*

The enemy likes to tickle your doubts and tantalize your flesh until you believe happiness comes through the fulfillment of your sexual desires. But nothing could be further from the truth. When we abuse God's original intention for our sexuality, the raw physical pleasure leaves us hungry and dry.

You have to let Jesus redefine happiness to find peace in your pursuit of purity. If you are willing to come to Him, to believe that what He promises you is better than the world, He will redefine your happiness and give you true joy—a joy that promises to satisfy.

In the book *Come Be My Light*, the editor, Brian Kolodiejchuk, wrote of Mother Teresa: "It was in giving Jesus whatever He asked that she found her deepest and lasting joy; in giving Him joy she found her own joy."[2]

Where will you find yours?

Refocus

I have loved you with an
everlasting love; therefore,
I have continued to extend
faithful love to you.

—Jeremiah 31:3

My husband and I just came in from walking through the trails of our pine-tree farm. It's winter so the wind has blown the dead leaves off the trees, and the weeds have wilted and fallen to the ground. Winter's cruel effect on the forest caused me to see things I didn't notice months ago.

I observed squirrels scurrying, a creek flowing through the trees, and our lone house, usually hidden by foliage, up on a faraway hill. Without all the weeds, leaves, and vines, I was able to see more clearly. But things had to die out to give me this perspective.

I've experienced my fair share of breakups. Immediately afterward, it seems like life will never be able to replace the devastation in your heart. It feels like a hurricane ripped through your heart. Maybe you find yourself lying on the forest floor, looking up at the bare limbs and smelling the decaying leaves as feelings of loneliness enter your heart and mind.

But before you go there, could I speak a little hope to your heart? I remember the tears of despair and breakup. I've entered *that* room where *that* guy stood across the room. You know, the one who chose not to stay with you or even give you a second chance. I know the feeling of wishing you were the other girl, the one all the guys fought over. Maybe you're wondering if something is wrong with you. Or perhaps you're convinced something *is* wrong with you, and you're frustrated.

Let's walk together in my woods. They seemed barren, dead, and desolate, but look again. They aren't. I can hear birds chirping and see the sun shining on the forest floor that is normally shaded by leaves. It seems like the forest should be colder and lonelier in the winter, but see how it's actually more open to your sight, to the sun?

It's the same when we're love lonely. We want a relationship to fix our empty hearts, but look around you. Wake up! It's time to refocus, not cover up your loneliness.

Look around. Who are you, and what are you experiencing?

When you're love lonely, you can more clearly see the condition of your soul because no one else is around to cloud your view. When you're love lonely, you have more room for Jesus to shine His love down on your forest floor instead of absorbing imperfect love from someone else.

Refocus.

When you're love lonely, it's the perfect time to receive and soak up God's love for you. See today's verse? When you're love lonely, you can hear these words a little louder.

Do you believe them? Can you hold them in your heart? If not, maybe you need time to.

DAY 27

Remember

Only be on your guard and diligently
watch yourselves, so that you don't
forget the things your eyes have seen
and so that they don't slip from
your mind as long as you live.

—Deuteronomy 4:9

Sometimes when you want to follow God, your heart may not keep beat with your actions. You plunge along the road of holy living because you know that what you are doing is right. Your actions line up with God's Word and instructions, but you're left feeling a little empty, lost, and lonely. This is when you start questioning everything:

- Why did I give my sexuality over to God?
- Why am I not dating *that* guy just because he isn't a Christian?
- Why am I waiting when NO ONE else is?
- Why am I waiting when I don't feel like it?

If you find yourself questioning, remember that the disciples experienced their share of doubts too. Jesus' death ushered them into one of the loneliest times in their lives. They'd given up their careers. They'd given over their hearts, hopes, dreams, and futures.

When Jesus was alive, their emotions motivated them to follow. They felt Him, they saw Him, and they trusted Him. But His crucifixion brought loneliness and disillusionment. They couldn't remember why they had followed Him, and this left the door open to doubt and questions.

- Why did we believe Jesus was different?
- Why did Jesus abandon us?
- Why didn't He fight for us?

Little did they know, He was resurrected. He hadn't left them. He hadn't abandoned them, and He did fight for them. But they didn't remember everything He had promised while He was alive.

Disappointed in Jesus, two disciples left Jerusalem, heading away from their Savior and their calling. A "stranger" joined them along the way who knew so much about the Scriptures that they shared their confusion and their sadness of Jesus' death with the stranger. They invited Him to dinner, and as the stranger broke a loaf of bread and offered it to them, they *remembered*.

They remembered all the times Jesus had served them bread. "Then their eyes were opened, and they recognized Him. . . . So they said to each other, 'Weren't our hearts ablaze within us while He was talking with us on the road and explaining the Scriptures to us?'" (Luke 24:31–32). In other words: "Why were we so blind on the road when He was talking to us? How did we not know it was Jesus?"

When Jesus was crucified, the disciples' emotions took over. Sadness and doubt clouded their eyes. They forgot what Jesus said, who He was, and their mission altogether.

Like them we can easily lose sight of *why* we are doing *what* we do. When your emotions are in conflict with the convictions you have about your sexuality, you have to *remember* why you are doing what you do, and the why is in the who.

Look beside you. Is a "stranger" trying to guide you back to the right road? Is He reminding you who you are and where you've come from? Is He reminding you that your life was worth His death? Is He reminding you that you are giving your sexuality over to Him because He loves you more than anyone else, because He has a more perfect love life planned for you than anyone else?

If you want successfully to dedicate your sexuality to God, you have to give the Holy Spirit command of your actions instead of letting your humanity dictate your reactions.

DAY
28

Repent

For you were called to be free, brothers;
only don't use this freedom as an
opportunity for the flesh, but serve one
another through love. For the entire law
is fulfilled in one statement: Love your
neighbor as yourself. But if you bite and
devour one another, watch out, or you will
be consumed by one another. I say then,
walk by the Spirit and you will not carry
out the desire of the flesh.

—GALATIANS 5:13–16

When we are sexually active outside of marriage, our bodies become sexually addicted. Close connection with our obsession keeps us from repentance. And passion to satisfy our habits keeps us from recognizing the devastation our behavior is bringing to our lives and to those around us. Paul warns against this behavior in today's verses.

When other people are involved in your sexual sin, you try to convince yourself that you're the only one hurting, but you're actually "devour[ing] one another" by keeping each other from repentance. When you "love your neighbor" and "serve one another through love," you treat others as children of God, honoring their calling to purity above your need for passionate fulfillment.

Repentance is a tool the Holy Spirit uses to keep us from gratifying the desires of the flesh. It takes humility and may be a little unsettling at first, but the freedom you experience as a result is invaluable.

When I was a little girl, I once went to bed with bubble gum in my mouth. I'm sure you know what happened. In the night the blob became one with a section of my hair. The blob wasn't easily removed. My wise mom rubbed and coated the mess with peanut butter until the gum began to loosen. The situation got messier before it got better, and finally the shampoo restored my hair to its normal condition.

Removing the gum in your hair is messy, embarrassing, and may take a little time. Repentance—getting rid of sin—feels the same. Don't avoid the process because you can't move forward with God until you have moved away from your sin. Repenting means you turn away from your sin and pursue righteousness.

Here are some practical ways to repent from sexual sin:

1. As soon as you have a lustful thought or act on a sinful desire, tell Jesus. Pray about it immediately and don't delay. The longer you wait, the harder it will be to repent.
2. Read, meditate on, and memorize Scripture that ensures you of God's willingness to forgive you.
3. Confess your sin to a trusted sister or mentor whom you respect.
4. Remember the process of repentance the next time you're tempted with the same sin as a way to avoid the same outcome.

5. Keep a journal where you write out your prayers of repentance and the verses that help you receive mercy. Here are a few:

- "Yahweh your God is among you, a warrior who saves. He will rejoice over you with gladness. He will bring you quietness with His love. He will delight in you with shouts of joy" (Zephaniah 3:17).
- "For Yahweh takes pleasure in His people; He adorns the humble with salvation" (Psalm 149:4).
- "The LORD is compassionate and gracious, slow to anger and rich in faithful love" (Psalm 103:8).

Repentance isn't easy, and it surely isn't fun, but it helps clear the path that leads us toward God and His purposes.

DAY
29

Replace

How happy is the man who does not follow the advice of the wicked or take the path of sinners or join a group of mockers! Instead, his delight is in the LORD's instruction, and he meditates on it day and night. He is like a tree planted beside streams of water that bears its fruit in season.

—PSALM 1:1–3

My kitchen recently experienced a remodel. But this didn't involve cabinets, tile, and countertops. Rather, I removed all the sugar, white flour, and canola oil and replaced them with Stevia, almond flour, and coconut oil. I changed what I ate and the way I cooked.

I didn't love the process. What sane person would choose to eat kale or spinach instead of a tasty blueberry-cake Dunkin' Donut? In fact, my taste buds often screamed in protest when I reached for a bag of raw almonds instead of a bag of sour cream and onion potato chips.

People said: "I could never do that. I admire your self-control." But I wasn't motivated by the desire to be self-controlled. For the last ten years, I had watched diabetes steal a loved one's life. Diagnosed in his thirties, he controlled his condition with medication but refused to change his diet. After ten years he became terminal, and each one of his organs shut down until he died in a hospice room.

He would miss seeing his children and grandchildren grow up, and they would miss his stories, laughter, and presence in their lives. This is why I started to make healthier choices. I determined that my family was immeasurably more important than a handful of doughnuts, Oreos, or chips.

You might be thinking: *Food is one thing, Sharie, but you're asking me to change my sexual desires. You don't know what goes on in my mind and body.*

I've watched movies about two people falling in love on that big screen with a boyfriend. My body temperature rose, my face flushed red, and my heart beat out of my chest while my thoughts and emotions ran wild. So, while I am not where you are now, I have been.

You are in a battle right now. You have God-given desire for intimacy, but you have to wait. An enemy wants to steal the treasure at the end of your rainbow. He will tempt you in your most vulnerable moment, just as he did Jesus.

After Jesus fasts forty days and nights with no food, Satan comes to Jesus and suggests He turn a few stones into bread. This would have been easy, but Jesus refuses to give in. He says, "It is written: Man must not live on bread alone but on every word that comes from the mouth of God" (Matthew 4:4).

Jesus could have produced a loaf of bread in seconds. In fact, He could have feasted on filet mignon. But when the temptation came to give up, to give in, He held out.

Why?

He had the future in mind. He only had three years before He would pay for sin while He was nailed on a cross. He knew victory would only come if He could train His body to replace its physical need with spiritual food. He was training His flesh for battle.

You are in a battle to let the gospel define your purity. Satan's purpose is "to steal and to kill and to destroy," but Jesus' purpose is to give you "life and have it in abundance" (John 10:10). Allow God to remodel and replace whatever is keeping you from the satisfying life He has in store for you.

DAY
30

Recommit

Accept my words, and you will live many years. I am teaching you the way of wisdom; I am guiding you on straight paths. When you walk, your steps will not be hindered; when you run, you will not stumble. Hold on to instruction; don't let go. Guard it, for it is your life.

—PROVERBS 4:10–13

When you find yourself tempted by sexual sin, you have to redefine, refocus, remember, repent, replace, and finally recommit.

If your dating relationships haven't honored God, you might decide to recommit your love life. Maybe you think, *I don't want to go that far sexually again*, or *I'm going to date a better guy next time*. Your heart is full of good intentions, but your recommitment lacks specificity and substance. To truly recommit you need to take time to examine your heart, pray about what went wrong, and let God show you how to change your behavior to get better results.

When I travel and speak, I meet a lot of girls suffering with bad-relationship syndrome. I usually challenge them to stop dating for a year.

Did you just gasp? Yep, I heard it.

Don't worry, I get a lot of that. Students often think, *I could never do that*, and their parents plead, "Don't challenge them to make a commitment they'll never keep." But consider my husband's wise words: "If you always do what you've always done, then you'll always get what you always got." If you don't change the way you're doing relationships, you won't get different results.

Time away from relationship drama gives you space to see God's perspective. He will help you see the mistakes you're making. What does He want to heal before you move on? Do you have any habits that are ruining your relationships? Do you need to look for a guy with different character traits than your past relationship choices?

In today's passage of Scripture, God declares that He will bless those who listen and obey His teaching, never letting it go.

God's promises to you are amazing, but they require commitment on your part. If you want God to honor His word, you have to surrender to Him. Take a minute honestly to assess your spiritual life. How long will it take for you willingly to surrender your relationships to God? How long before you're strong enough to hold firmly to Jesus and not be swayed by your friends or boyfriend?

For most Christians the process of listening and obeying God is lifelong. Right now a year may seem like forever. Later, when your relationships are healthy, you will consider it a small offering.

If you're afraid, don't feel alone. I've known a lot of people who were initially intimidated by this commitment (including me). But if I were to recount each person's miraculous life changes, we'd be here for days.

I pray that you will consider this challenge. I did it and haven't regretted it since. I'll be waiting to hear what God does in you!

Attention

Trust in the LORD with all your heart, and
do not rely on your own understanding;
think about Him in all your ways, and
He will guide you on the right paths.

—PROVERBS 3:5–6

Last year I took a flight to Thailand for a mission trip. I was surrounded by hundreds of other people who shared my claustrophobic and jet-lagged condition. We were trying to trick our bodies into believing these upright, unyielding airplane seats were designed for optimal rest.

As I sat dreaming of sleep, I realized that if someone hadn't had the courage to believe plane flight was possible, I might have spent weeks sailing across the ocean instead of taking a fourteen-hour flight.

I travel a lot, so it's easy for me to assume a plane will have enough speed and power to lift tons of weight into the air at the end of the runway. But that day I watched the Boeing 747 fill with people, luggage, gas, and supplies and marveled at the amazing ingenuity it takes to lift one of these giants off the ground. I don't have a working knowledge of aviation and gravitational science, but where my knowledge stops, my experience helps me believe in the inconceivable.

It takes guts to act on your faith. I wonder how many people bet against the Wright Brothers or thought Columbus would topple off the edge of the earth when he set his sails west. Benjamin

Franklin was surely signing a death certificate when he tried to harness the power of lightning, and Alexander Bell was surely crazy to think people could send sound through a wire.

Noah spent his months, maybe years, building a boat to save his family from a flood when a drop of rain had never fallen from the sky. And do you think people actually believed Mary was pregnant with the Son of God or that Elizabeth's son would usher in the Messiah?

We know none of these people were crazy because we've experienced the results of their faith. But I'm sure they received their fair share of criticism. In the midst of accusation, Columbus discovered a new continent, Ben Franklin harnessed electricity, and Alexander Bell invented the phone. Noah and his family were the only ones to survive the flood, and Elizabeth's son introduced the world to the Savior who came from Mary's womb.

As Christians we are called to dedicate every area of our lives to God, including our sexuality. This means we put aside the beliefs we've adopted from our experience and from our culture and instead make it our goal to understand and adopt Jesus' plan instead.

I know these words seem heavy and hard. Maybe the minute you read them, you felt like you were looking at a Boeing 747, thinking, *How could I ever make God's plan fly in my life?* It's my goal to give you the encouragement and faith you need to overcome. I've seen God's plan work in my life, and I believe it can work in yours. The key lies in taking the attention off our feelings, wants, frustrations, and overwhelming desires and placing our attention instead on who God is, what He has said, and what He promises when we are obedient.

I wonder how many times Noah's doubts dared him to stop short. Curious crowds with pointing fingers had to plant cries of confusion and chaos deep in his soul. But he traded in his own understanding for the ultimate One. If God's word to him was true, he couldn't build half an ark because it would never save him. He had to be all in if God was going to save him, if God was going to make his path straight.

One of my pastors, Shane Duffey, encouraged me with these words: "Believe more in the promises of God than the circumstance. God doesn't set us up to fail but to have faith—*so have faith!*"

FOR GIRLS

What will you dare to ask God for today? When we change our attention, we shift our affections and find the straight path that our hearts are longing for.

DAY 32

Affection

Love the LORD your God with
all your heart, with all your soul,
and with all your strength.

—DEUTERONOMY 6:5

FOR GIRLS

What do Pop-Tarts, pop stars, and popcorn all have in common? At first they seem fresh, but soon they are finished or forgotten.

Your affections behave similarly. They stir up your emotions, creating an immediate craving, which may or may not be long lasting. Your affections are a perfect source of motivation when properly applied. But misdirected affections take us in a dangerous direction.

When I was pregnant, my body craved pizza, Heath bar Blizzards, and chips and salsa. A commercial for pizza would appear on my television screen, and *boom*, my salivary glands went into overdrive as the cheese from the pizza stretched endlessly from slice to pie. If I let my mind linger, my belly began to rumble. My struggle felt unbearable. If I could get my hands on a phone, I knew my husband would have a pizza in my lap in half an hour.

But you crave what you consume.

I had to control my craving or I'd become a human baby blimp. So I limited my accessibility to these items and filled my cabinets with a more nourishing addiction: apples and peanut butter.

When the cravings came, my new obsession was within arm's reach.

The things you admire, obsess over, dream about, and talk about are the things you learn to love. So if you fill your heart and soul with shows, books, or Internet sites full of overdramatized romance, fictional love stories, or lustful affection, you will long to fulfill these fantasies in real life. Dreams, imaginations, and musings will no longer satisfy you. You'll soon hunger for the real thing.

The things that grab your attention will eventually capture your affection.

Focusing your attention on malnourished affection will lead your heart into temptation. If you want to change your craving, you have to find a new passion. And today's verse is the perfect place to start.

Let's be honest. It seems impossible to love the Lord with *all* your heart, soul, and strength. But if you are intimidated by the word *all*, could you start by making your affection for God a priority? When we aren't used to craving God, we have to train ourselves to do so.

So how do you do this practically? Earlier I described how a simple slice of pizza made my mouth salivate and my tummy rumble for food. If you're trying to love God more but you're watching things that take you into an unhealthy dream world, change what you watch. If you don't know if a show is good for you or not, a friend of mine always says, "When in doubt, don't."

As you're cutting out unhealthy cravings, you have to replace them with healthy ones. So many people tell me they don't have time to spend with Jesus, but if you cut out some unhealthy habits—voilà!—you'll have more time. Set aside time to spend with God. Write down Scripture or a quote that stands out to you during this time. Place it in a prominent place, like the mirror of your bathroom, so you can read it when you're getting ready. Post it on social media to instigate conversation with friends. Tell them who God is to you, how you are changing.

You can teach your brain what to think and your heart what to love, but you'll need discipline and consistency to get your affections right. As you redirect your affections, Jesus will support you. "For He has satisfied the thirsty and filled the hungry with good things" (Psalm 107:9).

Inspection

There is a way that seems right to
a man, but its end is the way to death.

—Proverbs 14:12

One time I washed a sweater that was meant to be dry-cleaned. I didn't realize my mistake until I switched my clothes from the washer to the dryer. I pulled out a baby-sized sweater, held it up, and wondered, *Whose is this?* Then I knew! Frustrated, I looked at the tag: "Dry Clean Only."

I muttered to myself, "I'll never do that again." But I did. After that I was even more determined to inspect my laundry closely. I didn't want to deplete my bank account or my closet.

When we make a mistake, we know logically that we should find a solution to keep this from happening again. So, why don't we examine our relationship mistakes the same way? Examine the problem. Find a solution. Easy, right? So, why don't we? Maybe because we wrongly assume that love and common sense are incompatible. We rationalize that love is about emotions, feelings, and passion while wisdom and common sense are cold and unfeeling.

So let me ask: What were your feelings screaming during your last breakup? Was it, "Don't do that again!"

You make illogical mistakes in relationships because your desire to love and be loved blinds you from past mistakes and deceives you into making them again. Maybe you hoped this guy, this time, will be different. Or maybe you're too scared to see the warning signs because you're already emotionally connected.

While this behavior is considered "normal" in our society, that doesn't make it unavoidable. Jennifer Rothschild says in her book *Me, Myself, and Lies*, "To understand the seen part of your life, you examine the unseen part."[3] In other words, mistakes you make are not as much about *what* you are doing, but *why* you are doing it. They originate from an internal deficiency rather than an external error.

You are hurting yourself over and over in relationships because you aren't taking time to look at your care tag. You probably aren't looking at the tag because you're afraid of what you'll see. But according to Proverbs 14:12, we need to examine our ways a little more closely because some of them are really harmful. This is why you need the Holy Spirit. He inspects your heart. He helps you uncover things in your heart that blind you and cause you pain. He does this because He loves you. He is trying to keep you from hurting yourself and the people you love. His job is to warn you of danger and imbalance in your heart.

When you're ready for the Holy Spirit's inspection, pray this: "Search me, God, and know my heart; test me and know my concerns. See if there is any offensive way in me; lead me in the everlasting way" (Psalm 139:23–24).

At first, inspection by the Holy Spirit may feel intimidating, unloving, cold, or sterile, but healthy relationships are the result of careful inspection. It's your choice: you can let your mistakes define you, or you can let them show you how to change.

Regular inspection leads to wise discretion.

Direction

The one who walks with the wise
will become wise, but a companion
of fools will suffer harm.

—PROVERBS 13:20

God hardwired you to connect with people on an emotional level. You need friendships—girls you can hang out with and talk to as well as older women who can give you advice, tell you stories of their own failures and successes, and coach you through tough seasons. You also need men in your life: a dad, a brother, uncles and grandfathers, and friends at church and school. You need to learn how to relate to guys, how to understand them, and how to value them as your brothers in Christ. Simply put, you need to be around people, and you need to belong to people in order to become the kind of woman God wants you to be.

With that said, sometimes it takes a little effort to find these people. My first day of college, I didn't know *anyone*. There were lots of people, but it didn't seem like any of them were headed in my direction. I tried to connect with people during the day, but it didn't seem to work. I rejected invitations to parties, dates, and drug circles. These invitations promised entertainment but not fellowship.

I needed fellowship so I tried to connect with people in class and in my dorm. It wasn't working. One night I was crying myself to sleep in my oh-so-exciting dorm room, and I prayed, "God, I'm trying to live life in Your direction, but I'm lonely. I don't know how much longer I can do this."

The next day I found a weekend invitation to go hiking with a campus ministry. I shoved it in my backpack, and three days later I was sitting in the parking lot thirty minutes early waiting for the caravan to arrive.

Jesus was faithful. I had the best day ever. The relationships I developed that day were indispensable during my four years at university. I found healthy male and female friendships and a special woman who mentored me. The treasure I discovered in this fellowship was worth a few days of loneliness and tears.

When you look back on your life, the friendships that last will be the ones that carry you in the right direction. Look for a friend who:

- Talks about Jesus with you and encourages your faith
- Accepts your true self
- Will work through disagreement and conflict
- Is consistent and forgiving

Using wisdom and discretion in relationships may be harder on the front end, but the benefit you will receive in the end far outweighs the struggle to get there. When you choose wise friends, their wisdom will make you wiser. But you can only absorb others' wisdom by spending time with them in real relationships.

Expectations

How can a young man keep his way
pure? By keeping Your word. I have
sought You with all my heart; don't let
me wander from Your commands.
I have treasured Your word in my
heart so that I may not sin against You.

—Psalm 119:9–11

I dated because:

- I wanted to make new friends.
- I was afraid to be alone.
- I thought I would be a good influence on his relationship with Jesus.
- I had a crush for years, and he finally noticed me.
- He was fun to be around.
- I needed a date for a dance, a prom, or another event.
- I thought it was God's will.

We date for many reasons. I've had a relatively mild dating experience with few regrets. But like most people I have a few that I wish I could wash away. I've often dreamed a time machine would show up on my doorstep so I could change a few situations. But I've changed my mind.

Instead, I think I'd take myself out for coffee and say, "Sharie, you wouldn't believe the amazing love story God has planned for you. But, if you'd like to avoid some heartache along the way, you need to sit down right now and decide what kind of guy you are looking for. Do you want a guy who encourages your faith or one who is embarrassed by your love for Jesus? Do you want him to share the commitment to purity, or are you going to choose someone who finds your goals absurd? Do you want a best friend or a fling? Set your expectations now because most relationship mistakes originate from our lack of vision."

You must decide what kind of person you are looking for before you start looking. Ask God to help you set a list of expectations. Expectations are your first line of protection against compromise.

Maybe you think having expectations is intolerant, rigid, and unkind. But if you ordered spaghetti at a restaurant and you got a slab of salmon instead, you'd probably send it back. If you interviewed for a position as a finance director but had a degree in psychology, they'd probably choose someone else. If a pro-football team kept losing, they'd fire the coach and find someone who could get the job done.

Living a sexually pure life is not easy. If you want to stay on this narrow path, if you want to glorify Jesus as His child, you have to set some expectations to make it work.

According to Psalm 119, you should both be:

1. Living according to God's Word
2. Seeking God with all your hearts
3. Open and willing for God to keep you from sin
4. Learning the Word of God so you can live by it

The above expectations are essential. Now take some time to set some personal ones and give your list to God in prayer.

DAY
36

Stand Up

Let no one despise your youth;
instead, you should be an example
to the believers in speech, in conduct,
in love, in faith, in purity.

—1 TIMOTHY 4:12

FOR GIRLS

The professor of my freshman seminar class encouraged each of us to pick up our package at the health clinic. We each had free access to condoms to protect us from various forms of STDs including the AIDS virus. Ironically, the headline of the school paper that day was, "Condoms Don't Protect against AIDS Virus."

I didn't want to embarrass my professor, but she was misinformed. So I slowly raised my hand to show her the article. Her countenance was filled with frustration and her eyes with scorn. In her mind she was "just trying to protect all these mindless, sex-crazed teenagers." But my heart was hurt by the assumption that her class was full of fornicators. I heard a few giggles as I shared my hope to honor God with my sexuality, but I also noticed a few who shared my commitment. The professor cut off the discussion with a condescending, "Good luck."

Not everyone will approve, applaud, or even believe in your commitment. Ridicule is often part of the package. But when you feel discouraged, God has given you these words to help you stand up for your beliefs: "Never let loyalty and faithfulness leave you. Tie them around your neck; write them on the tablet of your heart. Then you will find favor and high regard in the sight of God and man. Trust in the LORD with all your heart, and do not rely on your own understanding; think about Him in all your ways, and He will guide you on the right paths" (Proverbs 3:3–6).

People around you may not understand your calling. You may even doubt it yourself sometimes. But don't let doubt keep you from obedience. Let love and faithfulness to Jesus motivate you, knowing that you are living in God's favor. Don't forget that Jesus is worth your trust.

Just before graduation day I happened to see my professor for the first time since my freshman class. I approached her and humbly said, "I don't know if you remember me, but I was in your freshman seminar class. On the first day of class, we had a discussion about condoms, AIDS, and sex. I just wanted to let you know that I haven't been sexually active my entire college career. This may be unusual for you to hear, but I wanted to let you know that you may have more people like me in your classes—people who want to honor Jesus with our bodies—and it's working because we believe He can make it possible."

She responded, "Well I'm glad it worked for you," and walked on.

God has called us to stand up, to plant seeds of faith. If we never speak up, they will never know to believe. I don't know how these simple words affected her, but I choose to believe that God is using that seed today.

I pray that His love and faithfulness will allow the gospel to define purity to those around you who don't believe.

Speak Up

Then we will no longer be little children,
tossed by the waves and blown around
by every wind of teaching, by human
cunning with cleverness in the techniques
of deceit. But speaking the truth
in love, let us grow in every way into
Him who is the head—Christ.

—Ephesians 4:14–15

My junior year of college, I entered the classroom and sat in my normal seat. A guy who'd been flirting with me all semester started bragging about the girl he'd met over spring break. My apparent lack of interest led him to ask, "What kind of escapades have you been up to?" I told him that I'd gone on a retreat over spring break.

Then out of nowhere he said, "What are you, some kind of virgin?"

How "retreat" and "virgin" went together I still haven't figured out, but the room was silent. Embarrassed, I spoke softly. I was proud that I managed to speak at all.

"Yep."

There were wide eyes all around until he said, "Well, we will just have to call you 'V.'" Then he conducted a visual demonstration, holding up two fingers to form the letter *V*. From then on, every time he saw me, he'd salute me with a *V*.

I thought this would be the worst moment of my existence, but instead it became a positive, defining moment for me. As mortifying as the situation seemed, somehow I found freedom. First, the cat was out of the bag: my secret was out. Everyone knew where I stood so I no longer had to worry what people would say or think when they found out. They thought. They said. And I survived.

Second, my humiliation opened a door for me to share my faith with a few people in that class, and for some reason others came to me for relationship advice. Also, my sexual status earned me a position of honor and respect with my nicknaming fellow.

You never know what effect an honest answer may have on the people around you. Perhaps Jesus will use your "embarrassing moment" to surprise people into curiosity. It never crossed my mind that God would use my virginity to instigate an outreach.

What will He do when you speak up?

We've all taken different journeys with the Lord. I don't know where you are in your journey, in letting the gospel define your purity, but I know that each of us carries a different story of redemption and grace. If you're willing to speak up, I know God will take your testimony to plant a seed.

You may not be able to see what God is doing behind that person's protective mask, but if you have the courage to speak up boldly, the Bible makes you a promise. According to today's passage, it will—at the very least—help us grow closer to Christ. And that alone is worth the risk.

So be bold . . . and speak up.

DAY 38

Grow Up

Let us grow in every way into Him who is the head—Christ. From Him the whole body, fitted and knit together by every supporting ligament, promotes the growth of the body for building up itself in love by the proper working of each individual part.

—Ephesians 4:15–16

FOR GIRLS

I was motivated to go to church that morning, but I walked out of the service with my head down. I thought I understood what God expected of me, but as I sat in the service, I was shocked to find out there was an area of my life where I was sinning. Believe me, I didn't know I was sinning. I felt caught off guard, frustrated, afraid, and honestly completely inadequate to conquer this on my own.

I knew I needed help, so I spent the evening trying to confess, despite my incessant tears and sobbing. At the end of my blubbering, I looked into their eyes for encouragement and direction. But they blew me off.

They didn't share my burden.

They didn't feel like my sin was worth worrying over.

They tossed my request for guidance aside.

There was no follow-up.

No encouragement.

I lay in my bed crying and praying through my feelings of loneliness and confusion. Why would God convict me of something that was no big deal? Was He convicting me, or was I wrong? If these people didn't think it was a big deal, should I just give in?

I was confused and disoriented in my faith. In this moment I had to choose faith or doubt, to believe Jesus spoke to me or give in to my friends' ambivalence. I trusted God to help me overcome, and today I have no regrets.

Sometimes other people will not understand the growth Jesus is developing in your life because they are not growing.

Sometimes other people will not understand the conviction you are feeling because they don't allow God to convict them of sin.

Sometimes other people cannot hold you accountable because they haven't and will not give that area of their lives over to God.

Your desire to grow is inspired by the Holy Spirit. And as we grow closer to Christ, as it says in today's verse, it promotes growth and efficiency throughout the entire body of Christ.

So don't give up. Find someone else who is willing to feel, bear, or carry your burden with you. This is your heart, your walk, and your relationship with Christ at stake. This is your time to grow. Embrace it with all your heart.

Pray Up

Take the helmet of salvation,
and the sword of the Spirit, which is
God's word. Pray at all times in the Spirit
with every prayer and request, and stay
alert in this with all perseverance and
intercession for all the saints.

—EPHESIANS 6:17–18

Have you ever spilled your guts to someone, and they responded, "I'll be praying for you"? You're comforted for a moment, but then they walk away and you wonder if more important things stole their attention. Did they ever pray? Maybe their words were a spiritual way of saying: "I'll be thinking about you. I sure hope things work out."

I often promised to pray for people, only to forget about it later, until my friend Beth mentored me. We talked over coffee, but before we left, she grabbed my hands and actually prayed. If we were on the phone, she didn't say, "I'll be praying for you." She *prayed*.

At first it made me uncomfortable. Why didn't she just pray later? Well, Sharie, probably because she was so serious about praying for you that she simply *did it*. She believed her prayers made a difference so she didn't put it off.

The greatest weapon you have in your fight for purity is your access to God. When you turn to God for help, you invite Him into your vulnerable situation, and all of a sudden you realize you're not alone. His powerful presence takes the focus off your enticing thoughts and redirects them to Jesus.

The book of Psalms is full of prayers of desperation. David starts telling God about his fears and failures. He panics and pleads for help. But as the conversations continue, his focus shifts from his problems to God's presence. You can sense God's comfort when the psalmist recognizes God as his Defender, Deliverer, and Rescuer.

Prayer is your God-given tool. It activates the faith you need to be victorious against your temptations, fears, loneliness, discouragement, and shame. One of the most effective ways to pray is by using Scripture. This is how I pray using Scripture:

Jesus, You tell me that the woman "who endures trials is blessed, because when [she] passes the test [she] will receive the crown of life that God has promised to those who love Him" (James 1:12). So help me to persevere. Show me how to make it through this test.

Give me wisdom, because You say, "Now if any of you lacks wisdom, [she] should ask God, who gives to all generously and without criticizing, and it will be given to [her]. But let [her] ask in faith without doubting. For the doubter is like the surging sea, driven and tossed by the wind" (James 1:5–6). Tell me what to do in this situation. And when You do, help me to listen and obey. Thank You, Jesus."

This is how you fight temptation using Scripture and prayer together. Here are some other Scriptures I've found useful:

- Matthew 6:13
- James 1:2–4, 12–13, 16–17, 22
- James 4:7–8
- Mark 14:38
- Luke 11:9–10
- 1 Corinthians 10:13

Stay alert, pray, and you will find your way.

DAY 40

Don't Give Up

Everything is possible
to the one who believes.

—MARK 9:23

> Stop wondering if Christ can do anything in your situation and start believing Him to do everything glorious!
> —Beth Moore, *Jesus, the One and Only*

I've had a relationship with Jesus since I was eleven. I've tried to live a life that glorified Him, but looking back, I know I missed the mark sometimes. Many of my actions and words that I thought were holy and glorifying to Jesus were, well, let's just say they were learning experiences.

In Mark the disciples had their own learning experience. A desperate father asked them to help his boy who was possessed by a spirit. The spirit made the boy mute, often tried to throw him into fire, and threw his body to the ground where he would foam at the mouth and gnash his teeth. Jesus had given them power to heal and cast out spirits, but for some reason they couldn't help this boy. The teachers of the law pounced on the disciples' "failure," using it as an opportunity to attack the disciples with theological arguments.

When Jesus shows up, the chaos continues as the boy convulses and falls to the ground, foaming at the mouth. But instead of focusing on the boy, Jesus tries to pull the father's faith to the surface. Caught in panic mode, the only words this simple father can muster are, "If You can do anything, have compassion on us and help us" (Mark 9:22).

Jesus confounds the chaos with one clear statement, "'If You can'? Everything is possible to the one who believes" (Mark 9:23).

I served as a missionary overseas for three summers. I had the privilege of seeing a blind girl receive sight, a student's skin healed of hives, and a baby receive healing from a hole in his heart. I was not present for one of the most amazing miracles they witnessed, but I will never forget the story.

The team was holding services in a remote field when a desperate family showed up with their deceased son. He had been dead for hours. Still they pleaded with our leader, "Can you raise him from the dead?" The only response our leader could muster was, "I don't have faith for that." But the family placed their son under the stage, hoping for a miracle. Two hours later people approached the front of the stage for salvation, and the young man crawled out. He was alive.

When Jesus said, "Everything is possible to the one who believes," the boy's father confessed, "I do believe! Help my unbelief" (Mark 9:24).

Jesus heard the honest words of a father: "I want to believe that You can heal him, but I'm having trouble. Can You help me believe? Will You give me the faith so my child can be free?" Jesus responded by delivering the boy.

Sometimes your faith is hiding beneath your confusion and doubt. Maybe you believe it's impossible to be sexually inactive until marriage. Whatever your doubts, I plead with you, "Don't give up! Everything is possible for one who believes."

In both of the above situations, the men lacked faith. But they wanted to believe. So Jesus worked a miracle in spite of their doubt.

When I lack the faith to believe, I cry to God, "I believe! Help my unbelief," because faith to overcome doesn't originate in me. Rather, Jesus places His faith inside me, helps me find it, and teaches me to use it.

Jesus can override your doubt with His faith and one day present you pure and clean to that husband of yours. So don't give up!

notes

Day 24: Redirect

1. Phillip Clarke, Laura Howell, Sarah Khan, et al., *Usborne Mysteries and Marvels of Science* (Tulsa, OK: Educational Development Corp., 2005), 71.

Day 25: Redefine

2. Brian Kolodiejchuk, ed., *Come Be My Light* (Image, 2009).

Day 33: Inspection

3. Jennifer Rothschild, *Me, Myself, and Lies* (Nashville, LifeWay Christian Resources, 2010).

About the Authors

Sharie King was saved at the age of eleven and sensed God calling her to share her story of rescue and redemption. She has shared the gospel at Crossroads camps, college campuses, and mission trips in countries like Poland, India, and Malaysia. She is the vision developer and speaker for Clayton King Ministries as well as the founder of Ladies Only, the women's ministry division. Sharie speaks at women's events in local churches and conferences across America, teaching on marriage and ministry with her husband, Clayton. She also speaks on sexual purity, finding your identity in Christ, and overcoming fear. Sharie has a heart to see women embrace the truth of the gospel. She loves painting, writing, and homeschooling her two boys.

Clayton King is president of Clayton King Ministries and Crossroads Summer Camps, the teaching pastor at Newspring Church, and campus pastor at Liberty University. He is an evangelist, author, and missionary. Clayton began preaching at the age of fourteen and has traveled to thirty-six countries and forty-six states. He's written nine books and preached to more than three million people. Clayton is passionate about seeing people far from God repent of their sin and begin a relationship with Jesus. He loves to pastor pastors and empower Christians for ministry. He also loves four-wheelers, action figures, black coffee, and his wife and two sons.

For more information on Clayton and Sharie, their speaking ministry, or Crossroads Missions and Summer Camps as well as free sermons and resources, visit www.claytonking.com and www.sharieking.com.

The world is run by teen girls: parents of teen girls, teachers of teen girls, boys trying to date teen girls, companies trying to sell things to teen girls, and people who have had it "up to here" with teen girls. Chances are, if you're reading this, there is a young woman in your life for whom you desire the very best, and *10 Things for Teen Girls* can help with that.

Rooted in biblical wisdom and interspersed with candid stories of the modern teenage experience, these 10 important truths impart common (and all too uncommon) sense.

Available everywhere books are sold.

Available Now

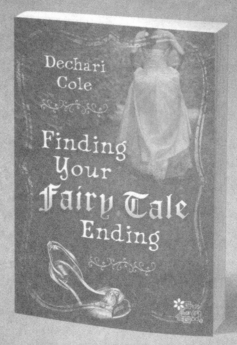

Aimed at encouraging "Girls to Live 4 God," author DeChari Cole shares the true story of a girl in search of happiness and love—a search that leads her through the wild and unpredictable world of friendships, dating, heartbreak, and loneliness.